the little
PLAY
BOOK

DR RUSSYA CONNOR & KATE HEASLIP

the book incubator

Published by the Book Incubator, 2023
Cover Design: The Book Incubator
www.bookincubator.com.au
Busselton, Western Australia

The Little Playbook text ©Dr Russya Connor
www.drrussyaconnor.com.au
Photo on facing page from author's private collection.

The Little Playbook illustrations ©Kate Heaslip

ISBN: 978-0-6454643-7-5

For Miro

Dear Reader,

This book has been written for you and for me.

It is a collection of personal notes that I want to share with you. Together, Kate and I have turned my scribbles into a playbook – a book for anyone who needs a little invitation to live a playful life.

Living a playful life means to think deeply and broadly, to fully embrace and experience our emotions, to be creative and to be open to a deeper awareness in the present moment.

Our darker emotions can be like a kaleidoscope. A rainbow of awareness, insight and creative discontent waiting to be unlocked. Playfulness will not magically change your reality or make uncomfortable feelings go away, but play will help you keep the flame of adventure alive.

The ability to be playful is most crucial when you feel alone, vulnerable, fragile or untethered in the world. When in survival or stress mode, our perception of reality narrows. We find ourselves repeating old patterns of behaviour, relying on set routines, and staying on established, predictable pathways. This leads to the most familiar (and inevitably least interesting) solution.

Being playful helps you to stay courageous, curious and resilient. It makes you less daunted when facing difficulties and less discouraged by disappointment.

Being playful reminds you of the benefits of having a joyful heart.

Being playful allows you to see wonder and beauty in the world.

When I feel like my joy is lost or new ideas become elusive and distant, I know from experience, that I need to play. Days can be flat. The absence of love can be heavy. Dread may lurk in the shadows and life can be scary.

I play.

Deep in my bones I know that I alone am responsible for my life. That knowing is frightening and exciting! I play to extract comfort, sweetness, beauty, pleasure, and adventure. Well, of course I can only speak for myself, but as it is working for me, I really wish from the bottom of my heart that some of these invitations also work for you.

With love,

Russya

jump in puddles

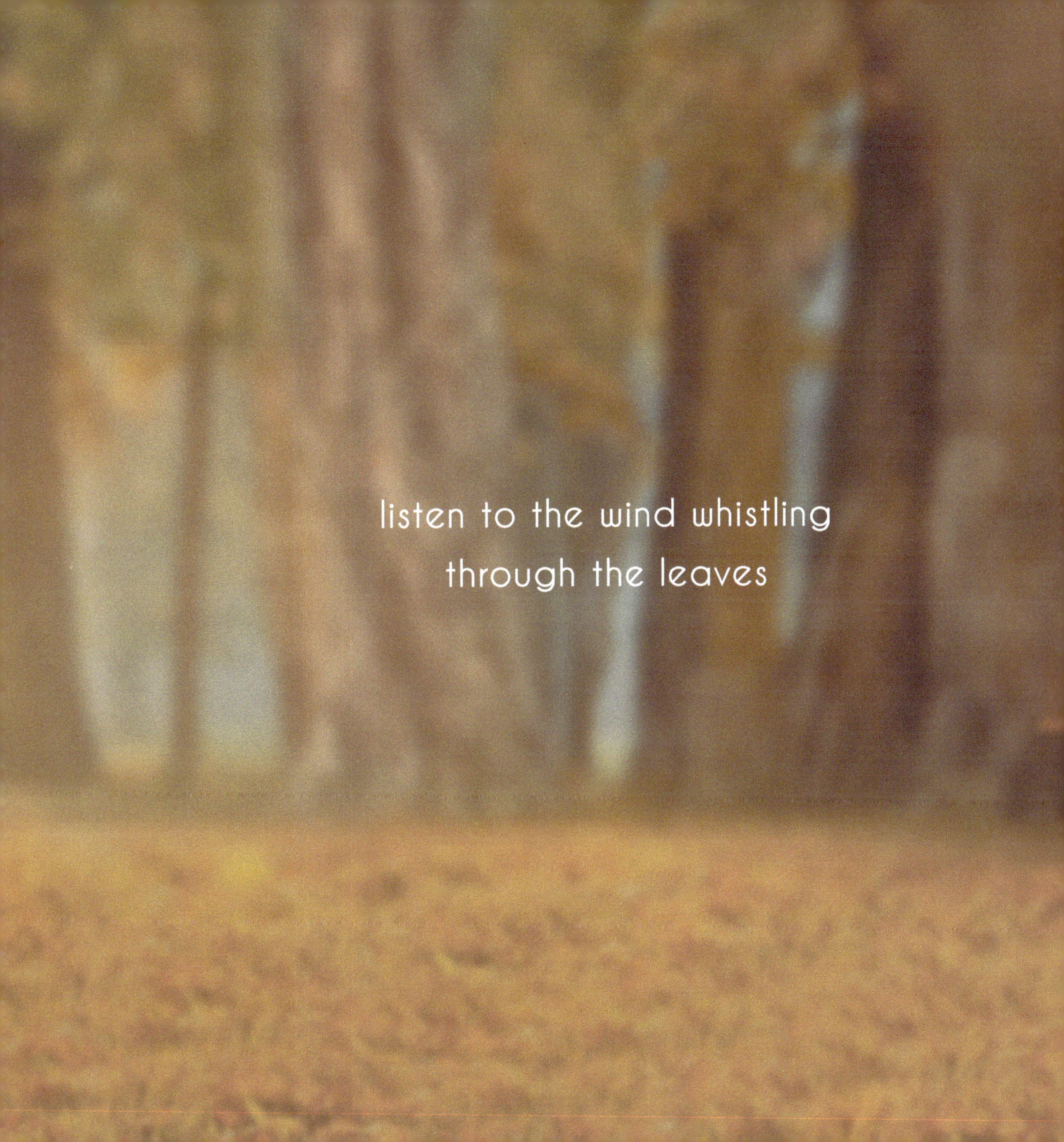

listen to the wind whistling
through the leaves

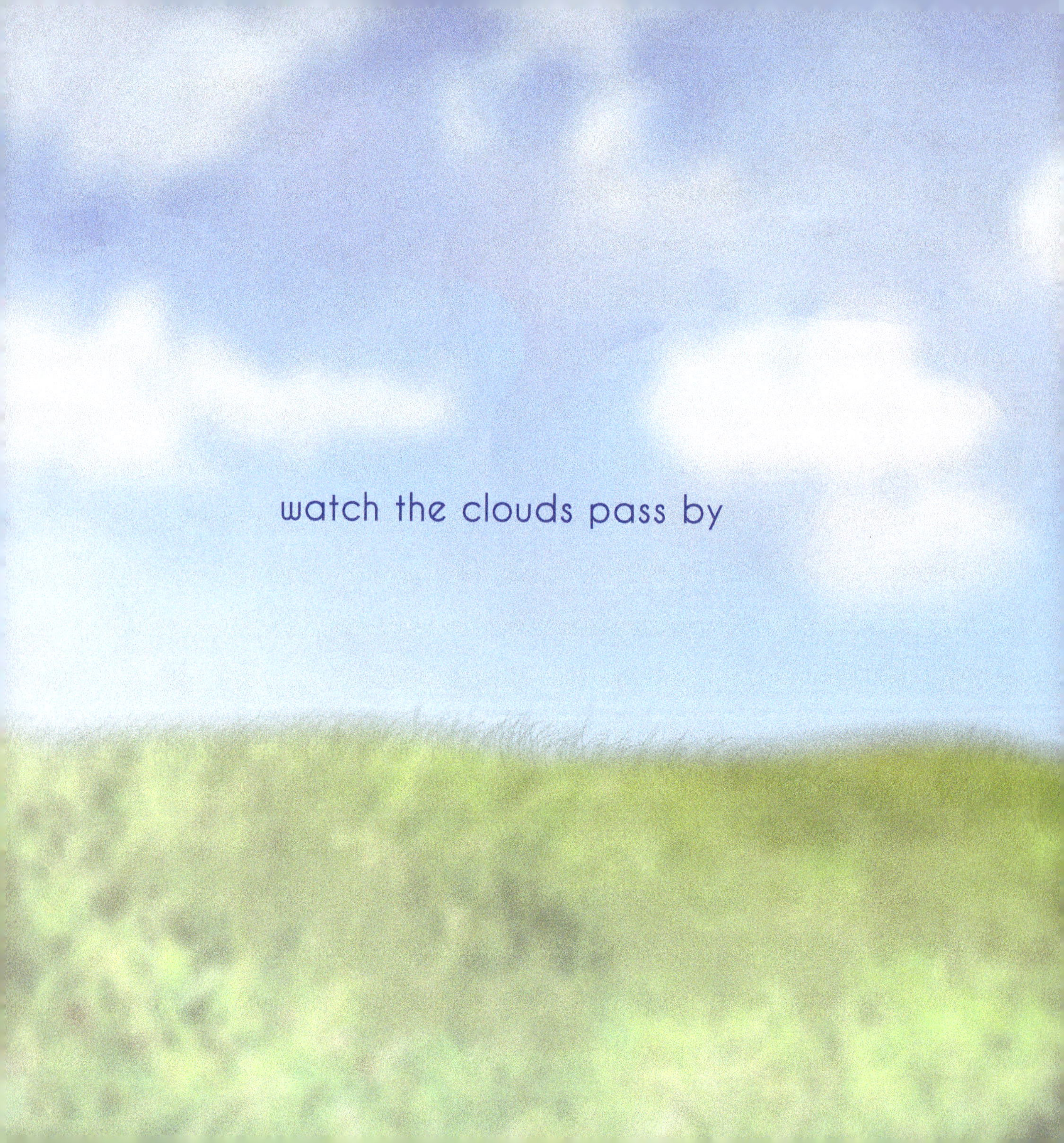

watch the clouds pass by

follow your curiosity

detangle your brain

make random

non-linear

asymmetrical moves

follow your own footsteps

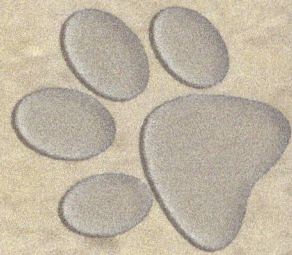

one step at a time

talk to a stranger

dig yourself a hole

gaze at the stars

dance in the moonlight

keep your heart and mind open

embrace the unpredictable

do something out of the ordinary

be deeply curious about someone else

come back home to yourself

nap in the late afternoon

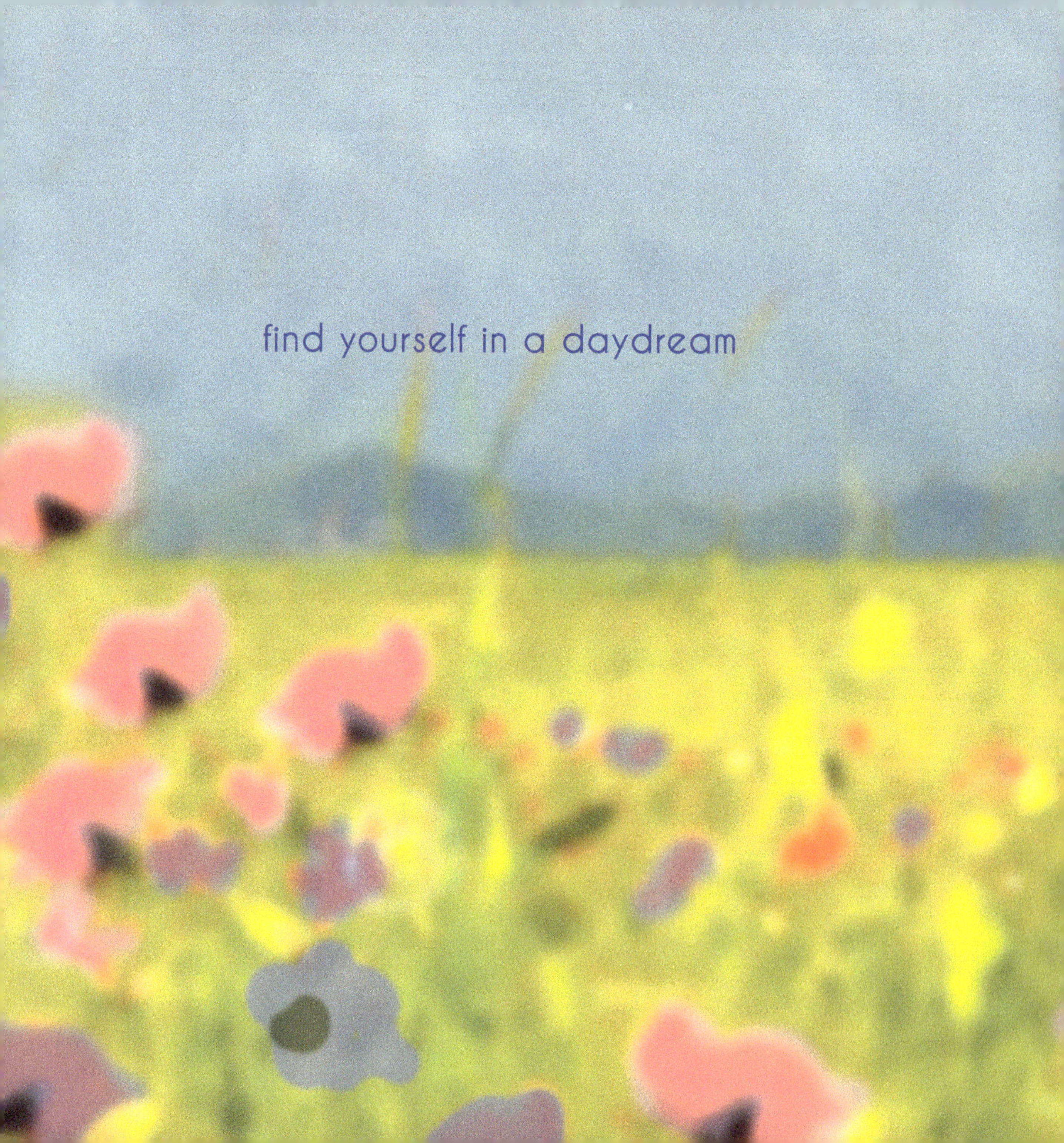
find yourself in a daydream

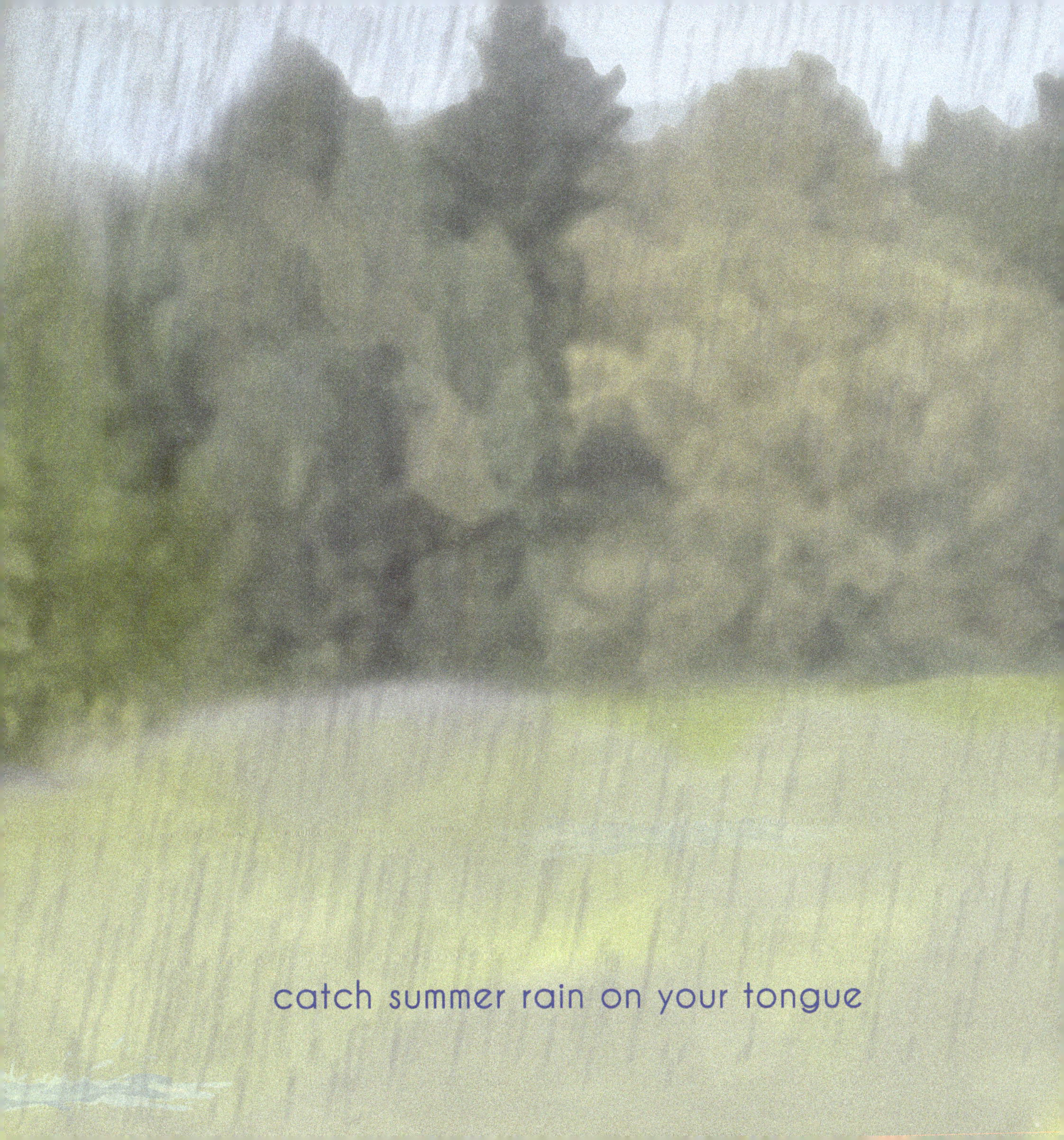

catch summer rain on your tongue

create millions of special moments

to chase the shadows away

change your perspective

create a small sculpture

break through the fear - take action

enjoy the absurdity of the moment

gravity always gets you

make a snow angel

enjoy a hot bath

pretend to be someone else

plant a flower or
even better,
plant a tree

be kind

share your pleasures

seek wonder daily

speak gently to yourself

if all else fails, howl at the moon

www.ingramcontent.com/pod-product-compliance
Lightning Source LLC
Chambersburg PA
CBHW060751150426
42811CB00058B/1369